D0429393

PABLO CASALS

Cellist for the World

92
CAS

David Goodnough

Enslow Publishers, Inc.

44 Fadem Road	PO Box 38
Box 699	Aldershot
Springfield, NJ 07081	Hants GU12 6BP
USA	UK

Library of Congress Cataloging-in-Publication Data

Goodnough, David.
    Pablo Casals : cellist for the world / David Goodnough.
    p. cm— (Hispanic biographies)
    Includes bibliographical references (p.) and index.
    Summary: Traces the life and musical accomplishments of the
renowned cellist and highlights his efforts as a crusader for world peace.
    ISBN 0-89490-889-8
    1. Casals, Pablo, 1876–1973—Juvenile literature. 2. Violoncellists—
Biography—Juvenile literature. [1. Casals, Pablo, 1876–1973.
2. Violoncellists.] I. Title. II. Series.
ML3930.C265G38   1997
787.4'092—dc21 92
                                         96-47792
                                             CIP
                                         AC MN

CONTENTS

STATE
DINNER

On the night of November 13, 1961, the White House in Washington, D.C., was ablaze with lights. Long limousines drove up the curving drive and stopped between the massive white columns. Women in long evening gowns and men in black tailcoats and white ties emerged and entered the gleaming mansion.

Inside, hundreds of people waited expectantly for the appearance of President John F. Kennedy and his wife. They were all here as invited guests to attend a state dinner given by the president for the governor of the Commonwealth of Puerto Rico, Luis Muñoz

Marín. There are many dinners and parties given at the White House by the president or his wife for personal or political reasons. A state dinner, however, is an official event sponsored by the United States government, usually to honor a visiting president or prime minister or other important person. But the real reason for this state dinner was to bring back to the United States the legendary cellist Pablo Casals.

Pablo Casals was one of the most famous musicians in the world. He was eighty-four years old, and during his lifetime he had played before most of the kings and queens of Europe. Sixty years earlier, he had played in this same mansion for President Theodore Roosevelt and his guests. He was Spanish, from the province of Catalonia, and for political reasons was in exile from his homeland. Years before, he had vowed never to play in public in any country that recognized the present government in Spain. Some of the people in the audience thought that he had broken his vow by agreeing to play at the White House since the United States still recognized the government of Spain. To most of them, however, this did not mean a thing. They had come to see the man and to hear him play music.

President Kennedy and Governor Muñoz Marín and their wives soon descended the staircase, and the assembled guests went in to dine. Meanwhile, Pablo Casals and his old friends, pianist Mieczyslaw

Pablo Casals (1876–1973) was an accomplished cellist, composer, and conductor.

Horszowski and violinist Alexander Schneider, were in the diplomatic waiting room. It was their custom never to dine before a performance but to have a small supper afterward.

After the state dinner, two hundred specially invited guests gathered in the grand East Room. Among them were diplomats, patrons of the arts, critics, and some of America's most notable musicians. Conductors Leopold Stokowski, Eugene Ormandy, and Leonard Bernstein were there, as well as composers Aaron Copland, Samuel Barber, Elliot Carter, Virgil Thomson, and Roger Sessions. The cream of American artistic and musical society was gathered into one room, and it was awaiting eagerly the appearance of one man.

A side door opened and a small, bald man appeared holding a cello, an instrument almost as tall as he was. His two companions seemed to tower over him. They took their positions at the end of the large room near the White House piano, a huge, nine-foot-long Steinway. President Kennedy rose and made a brief speech introducing Governor Marín and the three musicians. He spoke of the importance of the arts in a free society, saying, "The work of all artists stands as a symbol of human freedom and no one has enriched that freedom more signally than Pablo Casals."[1]

The president took his place in the front row of listeners, and the program began. It was a serious concert, unlike much entertainment at the White House. Usually White House dinners end with stage or film stars singing popular songs, dancing, or acting out brief skits. This was something else. It began with a piece by the German composer Felix Mendelssohn. "The moment Señor Casals drew his bow across the strings, it was with the power and authority he always has had," wrote one critic.[2] The musicians appeared nervous at first, but no one seemed to mind. In fact, the enthusiasm of the audience was such that they broke into applause between movements, which is not done under ordinary circumstances. The trio then played some concert pieces by the French composer François Couperin and ended with an adagio and allegro by the German composer Robert Schumann. The program lasted more than an hour. At its conclusion, Pablo Casals rose and said that he wanted to play a folk song from his homeland of Catalonia, Spain. He played *The Song of the Birds*, which was the unofficial anthem of all the Spanish exiles throughout the world. When he had finished, he walked over and embraced the president. It had been a moving performance, and the crowd was slow to leave, lingering with an "affection that played on the vanished scene."[3]

The first lady, Jacqueline Kennedy, had arranged a small supper for the musicians after the concert. Pablo Casals had a chance to exchange a few more words with the president, until an aide came and called

Pablo Casals performed in the East Room of the White House on November 13, 1961.

Kennedy away. "I am terribly sorry," said the president, "but there is a matter I have to attend to."[4] Mrs. Kennedy accompanied Pablo Casals and his wife to their car. It was a very cold evening and Mrs. Kennedy was not wearing a coat. Casals asked her not to accompany them outside, but she insisted: "The President would want me to—and I myself want to."[5]

Pablo Casals later wrote that "It was one of the most meaningful events of my life,"[6] for the president of the United States had assured him that he would do all he could to bring about world peace and freedom.

BARCELONA
AND BACH

Pablo Carlos Salvador Casals y Defilló was born in Vendrell, Spain, on December 29, 1876. Vendrell is a small town in the province of Tarragona, which is part of the region of Catalonia in northeastern Spain. It was only two and one-half miles from the Mediterranean Sea, in the hilly country just south of the large seaport of Barcelona. Although Vendrell was not cut off from the world around it, there were hardly any doctors in the village, and the nearest hospital was in Barcelona. So Pablo was born at home with only a midwife to help his mother.

A midwife was usually an elderly woman who had much experience in delivering babies. Pablo's birth was a difficult one, for he was born with the umbilical cord that connected him with his mother wound around his neck. He could have strangled if the midwife had not acted promptly and freed him. Pablo was his parents' second child. The first child, a boy named Carlos, had died earlier in the year that Pablo was born. It is not surprising, then, that Pablo became very special to his parents, especially to his mother.

Pablo's father, Carlos Casals, was born in Barcelona to a family that was in the business of manufacturing paper. Carlos Casals was very interested in music, however, and as a young man he was lucky to find work repairing old pianos. He also sang in a men's choir that he had started with his best friend, a barber named Peret. When Peret moved his barber shop to Vendrell, he found that the village's organ needed to be repaired. He arranged for his old friend Carlos Casals to come to Vendrell to do the work.

Casals liked the village and decided to settle in Vendrell. He soon became the village organist, choir-master, and piano teacher. He continued to sing in a choir and was a member of a small band that played at weddings and dances. Unfortunately, his health was poor and he had difficulty breathing due to an illness called asthma. Although he was considered an

important man in Vendrell, he did not make much
more money than an ordinary laborer.

Carlos Casals was interested in the politics of
Vendrell and Catalonia. He was a liberal, which meant
that he believed in a government chosen by the people
in free elections rather than one governed by a monarchy headed by a king or queen. He also believed in
self-rule for the province of Catalonia. Spain was then
governed by a republic, a form of government made up
of members of a parliament elected by the people. This
republic had been set up after Spain's Queen Isabella
had been forced to flee the country for political reasons
in 1868. It was a form of government of which Carlos
approved, but it still did not allow Catalonia to govern
itself. In 1874, the conservatives, people who believed
that Spain should still be under the control of the royal
family, attacked the liberal defenders of the Republic.
The Carlists, as the conservatives were called after a former leader named Don Carlos, passed through Vendrell
on their way to attack Barcelona. The people of Vendrell
prepared to defend themselves, and among them was
Carlos Casals. The townspeople were no match for the
Carlists, though, and were forced to flee to Barcelona.
Casals managed to separate himself from the defeated
defenders and make his way back to Vendrell. The experience made him a staunch liberal and a supporter of the
republic against the monarchy for the rest of
his life.

Pablo Casals's father, Carlos, was a politically active piano teacher in Vendrell, Spain.

Pablo's mother, Pilar Defilló, had been born in Puerto Rico. Her family had chosen to move to Spain to escape the harsh colonial government of their country. They settled in Vendrell, Spain, where Pilar's aunt ran a tobacco shop. The Defillós had led a comfortable life in Puerto Rico, but in Vendrell their standard of living was much lower. Pilar Defilló, however, was able to continue the piano lessons she had started as a child. Vendrell had only one piano teacher, and his name was Carlos Casals.

Defilló's mother died after a long illness, and she became the ward of her Aunt Francisca. This aunt disapproved of the young piano teacher, Carlos Casals. She considered him a dangerous political hothead, especially after he had taken part in the defense of Vendrell. When she found her young niece holding hands with her piano teacher during a lesson, she forbade Pilar to see Carlos again and canceled the piano lessons. Carlos, however, continued to court Pilar from afar. He even sang to her under her window at night, accompanied by Peret and the other members of his band.

Pilar's aunt eventually gave in, and Carlos and Pilar were married on July 16, 1874. Aunt Francisca did not attend the wedding, and Pilar entered her marriage without any of the privileges she had been used to as the daughter and relative of prosperous people. She gave away her elegant clothes and wore nothing but

Pablo Casals's mother, Pilar Defilló, moved with her family to Spain to escape the harsh government in her native country, Puerto Rico.

plain black dresses—as was only proper for the wife of a poor man, she explained.

The Casals family was not rich, but they were not poor either. The household was a happy one and, of course, was filled with music. Pablo later claimed that he was able to sing before he was able to talk and that musical notes were as familiar to him as words. His father was always preparing for his duties as church organist, for his singing group's concerts, and for his band's odd jobs. He also gave music lessons and included Pablo among his pupils. Pablo turned out to be an excellent student and soon was not only playing the piano but also writing simple music for it himself. When he was five years old, he began singing in the church choir and even composed some music for the church's Christmas program.

The family spent their vacations at the beach in nearby San Salvador, and Pablo learned to love the sea. He never tired of listening to the tales told by fishermen and the beach dwellers who were always ready to talk to the small boy. He was fascinated by the "unceasing flow of the sea. . . . I stayed for hours, resting my elbows on the windows watching this spectacle, always changing, yet always the same."[1]

His childhood was perfectly healthy and normal, except for the shadow of tragedy that seemed to cover the family. Pablo had a younger brother, Arturo, with whom he studied, played, and sang. Then, when

Arturo was almost five years old and Pablo seven, Arturo died from a spinal disease. This was to be a familiar experience in young Pablo's life, for no sooner was a new brother or sister born than he or she died at once or soon afterwards. By the time he was ten, Pablo had lost five more brothers and sisters.

Pablo learned to play the violin, the piano, and any other instrument he came across. He longed to play the organ, like his father, but the instrument was too large for him. It had to be played with both hands on more than one keyboard and with the feet pressing pedals beneath the bench. Pablo was a very small boy, and his father said he could not try to play the instrument until his feet could reach the pedals. "How I waited for that day!" Pablo later said. "I was never very tall, so the day took somewhat longer to arrive than it would have for another child."[2] It was not until he was nine years old that he could reach the pedals, but he quickly learned how to play the instrument. Soon he was taking his father's place at the organ during church services when Carlos Casals was ill or taking part in some other musical activity.

Despite all the time he spent on music, Pablo was able to lead the life of an active boy in the streets and fields of Vendrell with his friends and companions. Unfortunately, when he was ten years old, he was bitten by a dog that was infected with rabies, a deadly disease. In those days, there was hardly any hope for rabies victims, and they usually died. However, Pablo's father had heard of a cure for rabies that had been discovered by the French doctor Louis Pasteur just two years earlier. Carlos rushed Pablo to Barcelona, where there were hospitals and doctors who knew how to use this new antirabies serum. The serum saved Pablo's life. Pablo's mother, who had lost so many sons and daughters, thought that it was a miracle, and it endeared him to her even more. She became determined that her eldest son should have her care and protection above everything else.

Like other towns and villages outside the large cities, Vendrell had very little entertainment. There was no radio, movies, or television then. What the people had for amusement was either provided by themselves or by traveling groups of musicians and actors who gave performances in the town square. Pablo loved these groups, especially the musicians, who often played instruments they had made themselves. One such instrument that caught Pablo's attention was a crude string device. It was made from a broom handle and a cord of string stretched between two pegs. The player was able to produce melodies by pressing the string at different places with one hand while plucking it with the other. "For some reason," Pablo said in later years, "that broom-handle instrument fascinated me most of all."[3] Pablo begged his father to make him one. Carlos agreed to, but he made a much better one than the crude broomstick device Pablo had seen in the village square. Instead of a broomstick, Carlos used a hollowed-out gourd, which produced a louder and richer sound when the string was plucked. Pablo was delighted with it, and he was soon producing all sorts of tunes from it.

One day when Pablo was eleven years old, a much more professional group of musicians appeared in Vendrell. Among them was José García, a teacher at the Municipal School of Music in Barcelona. The instrument he played was a violoncello, or cello as it is commonly called. This is a stringed instrument that is much larger than a violin, and it is held between the knees while played. The rich tone that García produced as he drew his bow across the strings of the shining instrument captivated young Pablo. "I had never seen one before," he said many years later:

> From the moment I heard the first notes I was overwhelmed. I felt as if I could not breathe. There was something so tender, beautiful, and human——yes, so very human—about the sound. I had never heard such a beautiful sound before. A radiance filled me. . . . I told my father, "Father, that is the most wonderful instrument I have ever heard. That is what I want to play."[4]

He had found his perfect instrument, and he begged his father to get one for him. Carlos Casals, who might have objected to spending his scarce and hard-earned money on a toy or some other amusement

At the age five or six, Pablo Casals was already taking piano lessons from his father and composing music for his church choir.

for his son, could not object to a musical instrument. He obtained a three-quarter-size cello from the music school in Barcelona and gave it to his delighted son.

For the next few months, Pablo devoted himself to learning how to play the cello. His father looked on with interest. He was happy that his son loved music, but he never considered it as anything but a diversion for Pablo. Carlos knew how hard it was to make a decent living from music. He hoped to spare his son the difficulty and uncertainty of a musician's life. He had already arranged to apprentice Pablo in a solid trade that would always provide for him—carpentry.

Pablo's mother thought otherwise. She knew something of the larger world outside of Vendrell, and she wanted her son to experience it and make his mark in it. She noted his devotion to the cello and how well he played it. She saw in his playing a talent that could carry him much farther in life than skill in the craft of carpentry. She strongly opposed her husband's plans for their son, and the Casals household was split into two opposing camps, with the confused Pablo in the middle. He knew that he was the cause of his parents' arguments, but he was too young to have any say in the matter.[5]

In the end, the strong-willed Pilar Casals won out, and Pablo was enrolled in the Municipal School of Music in Barcelona. In 1888, the eleven-year-old Pablo and his mother took a third-class coach on the train to the capital. Barcelona was to be the first of the many great cities in which Pablo became a leading musical presence.

Pablo's father remained in Vendrell, since he could not afford to leave his job as church organist and music teacher. Pablo and his mother had to take a room in one of the poorer sections of Barcelona, but Pablo was thrilled with the great city. Although he had to spend most of his time at studies or practicing the cello, he and his mother still managed to visit the museums, libraries, and public celebrations of the city. Barcelona had been a great port city since the Middle Ages, and ships of all nations visited there, bringing with them the flavor and color of foreign places.

Only a few short weeks after they arrived in Barcelona, Pablo's mother had to return to Vendrell. She was expecting her ninth child and could not afford to have it in Barcelona. In the meantime, Pablo stayed with friends of his family, Benet and María Boixados. The Boixados family was fond of Pablo and treated him well. Benet made a great impression on Pablo, for he often talked about him later in life. It seemed that Benet was an enemy of all evildoers in Barcelona. After work, he would patrol the worst areas of Barcelona, armed with a heavy stick, to discourage any acts of thievery or violence. One night he was wounded by some thugs, and he proudly displayed the scar to Pablo.

Pablo was enrolled in a five-year course of study at the School of Music. His teacher was José García, the same man he had seen and heard play the cello in Vendrell. García was a fine teacher, but he played the cello according to the custom of the time. This meant that he played with the bow held stiffly and with his arm kept close to his side. Students were made to hold a book under their arm while playing so that their upper arm would not stray from position. Pablo, who had taught himself to play and took the arm position that was most comfortable to him and which produced the best tone, objected to his teacher's way of playing. Luckily, García did not object to change and allowed his student to stick to his own method of playing. Pablo also experimented with the left hand, which controlled the pitch and vibrato of the instrument. (Pitch is the location of a note on the musical scale, whether high or low. Vibrato is the pulsating effect that gives feeling or warmth to a note that is held for a length of time.) The approved method of changing pitch on the cello was to slide the fingers from one note to another when the interval, or distance between notes, was more than three tones. The sliding fingers created an unpleasant effect that even the most skilled players could not hide. Pablo worked out a way of extending his little finger to the higher-pitched note and then following it with his other fingers, thus getting rid of the sliding noise. This method was to change forever the way the cello was played. Pablo would always express his thanks to the man who allowed him to develop his own way of playing this difficult instrument.

At the School of Music, Pablo also studied harmony, which means combining two or more notes to sound at the same time. He also studied composition, or the writing of music, which was easy for Pablo since he had been doing it since he was five years old. He took these extra courses to make himself a complete musician and not merely a performer. He wanted to prove himself to his father, who still scoffed at his ambition to become a musician. To help with expenses and also to learn as much as he could about all types of music, Pablo found a job playing with two other musicians at the Café Tost in a suburb of Barcelona. The music they played included popular songs, dances, and selections from light opera. Pablo convinced the owner of the café and his fellow players to put aside one night of the week for serious music—in other words, a concert. The owner agreed, and the concerts were a great success. They attracted many people from other parts of the city who would not normally visit the café. Pablo's mother had returned to Barcelona after the birth of her ninth child—who died shortly after being born—and she attended many of the concerts. She was very pleased with her son's performance and the crowd's acceptance of him. She decided to permit him to travel with other musicians throughout the city to play at weddings and dances, just as his father had done when he was young.

Carlos Casals begged his wife and son to return to Vendrell, but with no success. He made the trip to Barcelona as often as he could, and on one trip he presented Pablo with his first full-size cello. Pablo remembered the day clearly, for it was then that he made a remarkable discovery. He and his father decided to visit second-hand music shops to try to obtain sheet music of new pieces that Pablo could perform at his café concerts. In one shop, they found an old edition of *Suites for Unaccompanied Cello* by Johann Sebastian Bach. The music of Bach was familiar to Pablo through the *Well-Tempered Clavier,* a series of short pieces for keyboard that his father had set him to playing on the piano as exercises. The cello suites were also considered exercise pieces by the few cellists who bothered to play them, and few had ever attempted the whole set of six. Pablo, however, was fascinated by them. He recognized them for the great music they were, perhaps the greatest ever written for his instrument. "I took the suites home and read them," he wrote many years later. "They were to become my favorite music. For twelve years I studied and worked every day at them, and I was nearly twenty-five before I had the courage to play them in public."[6]

Among the many people who made the trip to the Café Tost to hear "the boy cellist" was the composer and pianist Isaac Albéniz. He was so impressed with Pablo's playing that he took Pilar aside and urged her to take Pablo to London to play before a large and knowing public. Albéniz had been a child performer himself, and he knew that music-mad London was the place for a young musician to make his mark. Pablo's mother refused—she had heard what disappointments lay in store for talented children who gained success and fame only to lose it when they grew older. She also dreaded being separated from her oldest surviving child. Although she had another son, Luis, she still considered Pablo as a gift of God who must be protected as well as treasured. She even left Luis in the care of a family in Vendrell so she could be with Pablo in Barcelona.

Albéniz still wanted to help the boy, so he gave Pilar a letter of recommendation to Count Guillermo de Morphy, a well-known patron and friend of musicians. De Morphy also happened to be an adviser to the queen of Spain, María Cristina. There were no strings attached—Pilar was free to do with the letter as she wished. She decided to put it away for safekeeping, and perhaps for later use.

Pablo had been studying the cello for three years at this point and had become as fine a cellist as there was in the School of Music and, indeed, in all of Catalonia.

Spanish composer and pianist Isaac Albéniz was the first prominent musician to recognize Casals's talent and to offer him help in his career.

At the end of each school year, he was regularly awarded first prizes in performance and composition. He also took part in all year-end concerts. His mother decided it was time for his first real concert, playing serious music alone and in front of a knowing audience. So, on February 23, 1891, Pablo carried his cello, which was almost taller than he was, onstage at the Teatro de Novedades in Barcelona. He was fourteen years old and frightened. His head ached and he was sick to his stomach—until he was finally seated and began his program. It included Estévan Tusquets's difficult *Allegro Appassionato,* which Pablo played from memory. He received a standing ovation from the audience. The next day, the Barcelona newspapers praised his playing and intonation, or accuracy in producing pitch, and reported the audience's ovation. It appeared that the future of "the boy cellist," or "The Tost Kid," as he was sometimes called, was assured.

Despite Pablo's success at school, his father still objected to his wish to pursue a musical career. He argued that there were thousands of talented performers and composers in the world outside of Vendrell and Barcelona, and only a few of them were able to make a living for themselves and their families. What Pablo needed was a solid trade, such as carpentry, that would see him through good times and bad. Pablo's mother disagreed strongly with her husband and insisted that Pablo's future lay in the world of music.

Pablo's father finally gave up trying to get Pilar to move back to Vendrell, so he joined her and Pablo in Barcelona. He brought Luis with him, so they were a family once again. Carlos managed to find a few students who needed piano lessons, but money was always scarce. Pablo found a new job playing in a trio at La Pajarera (The Birdcage), a café that had just opened and had become a popular night spot. Pablo repeated his success from the Café Tost, and soon he was meeting and mingling with all the visiting musicians who made Barcelona a stop on their tours.

One of these was the composer Enrique Granados, who took a liking to Pablo. Granados was determined to create a Spanish opera that was in the great European tradition. In Spain, the *zarzuela*, a type of play with music, was the most popular form of musical drama. Pablo encouraged Granados in his efforts to create a national opera. In preparation for the first performance of his opera *María del Carmen*, Granados, who was shy and nervous, asked his fifteen-year-old friend to explain his new music to the orchestra. Other important musicians also relied on Pablo's musicianship. Camille Saint-Saëns, the famous French composer, asked Pablo to perform his *Cello Concerto* and said that Pablo's performance was the best he had heard. None of this made any impression on Pablo's father, however, and Pablo felt further estranged from him.

There were heated arguments in the Casals household that Pablo could not help overhearing. He became deeply depressed, feeling that he was the reason for his parents' fighting. At fifteen years of age, he found himself in the center of a family argument that he could do nothing about. Other matters also weighed heavily on his mind. Through the influence of his father, he was deeply patriotic and proud of his Catalonian heritage, but Catalonia was still under the control of Spain. From his experience in the music halls and his touring with traveling bands, he had seen the great differences in social classes and in the lives of rich and poor people. He was deeply religious, but the Church did not seem to care about or have any effect on the injustice of the society he saw around him. As he admitted later, he even thought of suicide as a way out of his deep depression and despair at the human condition. "Everybody has an epoch of distress," he said in later life. "I had it very young. It lasted a long time. It made me physically ill. . . . It was terrible."[7] There was only one thing he could turn to that had never failed him and that seemed to be his only refuge in his troubled world—and that was music.

Pablo graduated from the Municipal School of Music in 1893. He had won all of the prizes in composition, piano, and cello. He had now learned a large number of cello concertos as well as popular and semi-classical works that he had picked up in his work in

_French composer Camille Saint-Saëns considered Casals the finest interpreter of his works for the cello and actively promoted his career.

cafés. His teachers and his mother agreed that he should go on to further study in Paris, which was then the musical capital of the world. He entered a competition for a scholarship offered by the Barcelona City Council for study abroad. He was shocked when the prize went to another student. The judges may have thought that his method of playing was not proper for someone who was to represent the City of Barcelona abroad. Whatever the reason, his failure plunged Pablo into further gloom and depression.

He desperately wanted to leave Barcelona and his difficult family situation. His mother agreed, and even though her husband objected as usual, she decided to take Pablo to Madrid, the capital city of Spain, where he could be introduced to a wider musical culture. It was time to use Isaac Albéniz's letter.

COURT AND
CAREER

Pablo's mother could not imagine leaving her other children in the care of strangers, so she boarded the train to Madrid with Pablo and her two younger sons, Luis and Enrique. The journey took twenty-four hours. When the train arrived in Madrid, Pilar took her three sons directly to the home of Count Guillermo de Morphy. The count knew of their coming from Albéniz and welcomed them warmly. He immediately asked Pablo to play for him, and he was impressed by the young man's talent and obvious feeling for the music he was playing.

Count de Morphy was an Irishman whose family had fled political troubles in his homeland and had settled in Spain. They changed their name from Murphy to Morphy to appear more Spanish. He was wealthy and well educated and had become a friend and adviser to the Spanish royal family. At that time, the royal family was headed by Queen Mother María Cristina, the mother of the young King Alfonso XIII. Both de Morphy and the queen were lovers of music and were always on the lookout for Spanish-born musicians who could advance the cause of Spanish music throughout the world. De Morphy arranged for Pablo to play before the royal family in a private concert of chamber music. One of the pieces played was a composition by Pablo himself. Queen María Cristina was delighted with the young cellist and awarded him a scholarship to study at the Madrid Conservatory of Music.

Pilar settled her family into a small apartment across from the royal palace. Pablo's scholarship was for 250 pesetas (fifty dollars) a month, which was "not such a small amount then," wrote Pablo many years later. "In fact, it was quite a handsome sum in those days. Even so, it was not a great deal when it came to meeting the needs of a family of four. We lived very poorly."[1]

At the conservatory, Pablo studied composition and chamber music. The director of the conservatory,

Jesús de Monasterio, encouraged Pablo to pursue his own interpretation of the great music he was studying. Pablo later said that next to his father Monasterio was "the greatest teacher one could have had."[2] His general education was taken over by Count de Morphy, who believed that a complete musician should have a well-rounded education in order to achieve "a full understanding of life."[3] Pablo was taught literature, history, mathematics, and languages, all of which he would continue to study and use throughout his long life. He took advantage of the great Prado Museum to study the works of the European masters of art. He was encouraged to learn about government by sitting in the visitors' gallery of the *Cortes*, the Spanish legislature, and listening to the debates on the issues of the day.

In his spare time, Pablo played chamber music with his friends and fellow students. Sometimes they traveled outside of Madrid to give concerts in the towns and villages of the countryside. These concerts were always a big event to local inhabitants and attracted mention in newspapers that were eager to report on anything notable or unusual. One reviewer singled Pablo out for special praise. "At barely eighteen years old he can proclaim himself *Maestro*," he wrote. "When he plays, one closes one's eyes and hears, more than a work of art made by human hands, music that seems the miracle of a spirit."[4]

Pablo was often invited to play at the nearby royal palace, where he had become a favorite of Queen María Cristina. The queen was a musician herself and sometimes she joined Pablo in playing duets on the piano. The young king Alfonso XIII, who was then seven years old, would play on the floor with his collection of toy soldiers, and sometimes Pablo would join him before returning to his home across the street. Queen María Cristina was so pleased with the young Pablo that she awarded him a medal, the Order of Isabel la Católica, which was a great honor for an eighteen-year-old musician who had yet to make his mark in the world.

Pablo's success at the conservatory and in public concerts affected Pilar more than it did Pablo. She had been the first to recognize his passion for the cello, and it was she who had encouraged his study of the instrument. She was now disappointed that Pablo was not receiving the best instruction in Madrid. She decided that Pablo should go to Paris for further study. It was only in Paris, she thought, that a talent such as Pablo's would be appreciated and improved by the world's greatest teachers. There was also the opportunity for him to appear as soloist with the world's greatest orchestras and musical groups, which was the surest way to fame in the music world. Count de Morphy, however, had other plans for Pablo. He had long hoped for a national opera in Spain, written by Spanish

During his lifetime, Pablo Casals traveled widely to study and perform music. In this photograph, Casals plays in an artist's studio in Holland in 1907.

composers in the Spanish language, and he wanted Pablo to pursue that goal. Pilar said, "I believe that with Pablo the cello comes before everything else. If his future is to be that of a composer, it can always come later, and his work on the cello won't interfere."[5] Pablo's father, of course, argued that there were hundreds, even thousands, of talented musicians in Paris, and Pablo would only be lost in the shuffle. Once again, Pablo found himself in the midst of a controversy over his future.

Count de Morphy finally proposed a compromise. He suggested that Pablo go to Brussels, Belgium, where there was a conservatory with fine teachers in both the cello and composition. There Pablo could study both without the fierce competition of Paris. He assured Pilar that the queen's scholarship would be continued if they agreed to go to Brussels. That settled the matter, and once again Pablo, his mother, and two younger brothers made the long trip to a strange new city.

IN THE GREAT WORLD

Brussels was a disappointment. The cold and damp northern city with its dark, crowded streets was entirely different from the sunny towns and villages with open plazas and nearby countryside of Casals's youth. Count de Morphy had written a letter of introduction to the director of the conservatory, and Casals was promptly enrolled there. Much to his disappointment, however, he learned that the aged director, who was also the teacher of composition, was too old and frail to take on any new students. After looking over several of Casals's compositions, he suggested that he go to Paris for further study, but Pilar pointed out that they would lose their grant from the queen if they did. The director saw the truth of their situation and arranged for Casals to meet the senior cello teacher, Edouard Jacobs.

The next day, Casals arrived at the conservatory only to find that Professor Jacobs was already leading a cello class. Casals sat in the rear of the classroom and observed the lesson in progress. He was not impressed. He noted that many of the students were playing out of tune and making mistakes that the teacher failed to correct. All of them played in the traditional fashion with their arms close to their bodies. He was amazed, because he had been led to believe that this class was one of the best in all of Europe!

When the class was nearly over, Professor Jacobs appeared to notice Casals for the first time, although he had been sitting there for most of the class. "So I gather you're the little Spaniard that the director spoke to me about," he said. "It seems you play the cello. Do you wish to play?"[1] He asked if Casals had brought his cello, and Casals had to admit that he had not. He had thought that the meeting was to be only an interview, not an audition. When asked if he could play on a borrowed one, he agreed to play any composition the professor wanted.

Jacobs was amused. "It seems that our young Spaniard plays everything," he said. Then he named some difficult cello pieces by various composers. Casals nodded yes to everything that was mentioned. "He must be really quite amazing," teased the professor, and the rest of the class snickered. "Perhaps you will honor us by playing the *Souvenir de Spa,*" he said, naming a very difficult piece. Casals, however, knew the piece well and picked up the bow confidently, even though he was irritated by the teacher and the class.

Once he began playing in his own style, with his arms moving freely and his fingers stretching and sliding easily up and down the strings, the teacher and the class fell silent. When he had finished, Professor Jacobs did not say anything for a while but then dismissed the class and asked Casals to see him in his office. When they were seated, the professor without any hesitation told Casals that he had a great talent and that if he agreed to study with him at the conservatory, he could guarantee that he would be awarded first prize for the year's work. "It's not exactly according to regulations for me to tell you this at this time, but I can give you my word." This was an amazing turnaround by the pompous professor, but Casals was having none of it.

"You were rude to me, sir," he said. "You ridiculed me in front of your pupils. I do not want to remain here one second longer." The professor was once again speechless and could do no more than watch as Casals left the room. The great Edouard Jacobs was left to ponder his mistake at offending the greatest student he might ever have had the privilege to teach.

When Pilar heard what had happened at the conservatory, she agreed with Casals that he should not return. Not only had Casals been angered by his treatment by Edouard Jacobs, but he was disappointed in the quality of the instruction he had seen. It was settled: Paris was the place for Casals to continue his education. Once again, Pilar packed up their meager belongings and herded her small family of four onto a crowded train coach and headed for Paris.

In Paris, the family found lodgings in one of the poorest sections of the city. Pilar had written to Count de Morphy to explain the situation, but the count did not agree that the situation in Brussels was impossible. True to his word, he cut off their grant of money from the queen. He would not give Casals more money unless he agreed to return to Brussels. Neither Casals nor his mother spoke much French, and they did not have the backing or introductions of influential friends, so they found it difficult to find employment. Casals finally found work through a Catalan friend at a music hall, the Folies-Marigny, where he played in a band while can-can dancers did their act on stage. His pay was hardly enough to support a family of four, so Pilar was forced to take any work she could find. Casals was pained to find her working late at night on the piles of sewing she had collected during the day. One day he was horrified to find that she had cut her beautiful long hair and sold it to a wigmaker for extra money. "It is only hair," she said, "and hair grows back."[2]

Carlos Casals was unable to send them any money. Spain was then engaged in a series of wars with rebellious colonies in Cuba and Puerto Rico, and the government had increased taxes in order to pay for the wars. Hard times had hit Catalonia, and Carlos had lost many of his students. In addition, his health had taken a turn for the worse. Nevertheless, he sent them the last of his money for train fare back home.

By this time, winter had set in, and Casals fell ill from the cold and the long hours spent trudging to and from work at a job he did not enjoy, even though it involved music. When his father's money for the fare to Barcelona arrived, they decided to return home. Carlos was delighted to see his family again, but their prospects were not very encouraging. He had spent all of his savings and was barely managing to get by. Casals celebrated his nineteenth birthday that winter of 1895 and realized that he was now the main means of support for his family.

The situation suddenly turned for the better when, in January 1896, Casals learned that the Municipal School of Music was without a teacher of the cello. His former teacher, José García, had been forced to resign due to a scandal, and was moving to Argentina. Casals applied for the job and was accepted. He was also able to take over the duties as organist at church services and inherited García's former students as well. Casals loved teaching and was soon instructing his students in the easier, more fluid technique that he had developed. His students responded well, and his reputation spread. He was offered a second job at another music school, which he gladly accepted. He was now working constantly at doing what he loved, and the long hours at work flew by.

It was while teaching in Barcelona that Casals became aware of Catalonia's great musical and cultural institution, the monastery at Montserrat, located about forty miles northwest of the city. This monastery had been in existence for more than a thousand years, and one of the tasks that its monks performed was preserving the religious and folk music of Catalonia. Casals became acquainted with the monks of Montserrat and spent many hours visiting and discussing music with them. Although Casals had little interest in the outward show of formal religion, he composed a great deal of church music. Most of it was dedicated to the monks at Montserrat, and it is still performed by them regularly as part of their services. For most of his life, Casals never allowed any of his music to be published except as part of the musical library of Montserrat.

Now, for the first time in his life, Casals had money enough to spare, and he moved his mother, father, and two brothers into a comfortable house along a spacious plaza in Barcelona. He began to save his extra money to build a fund for his return to Paris. He now realized that it was there that he must make his mark. He would soon be twenty years old, which was rather old for a virtuoso instrumentalist to make his international debut.

Unfortunately, Spain was still involved in its wars in Cuba and Puerto Rico, where revolutionary parties were trying to gain independence from Spain. All able-bodied Spaniards over the age of eighteen were expected to serve in the army. Casals received his draft notice soon after he had moved into his new home. He consulted with his parents and without hesitation they recommended that he do everything he could to avoid service in a useless war. Carlos especially had no love for the Spanish Army and the royalist government that it served. Pilar, whose family had suffered at the hands of the colonial government in Puerto Rico, was deter-mined that none of her sons would ever serve in an army that supported such a government. At that time, it was possible to buy your way out of army service, and Casals had the money to do it. Unfair as this may seem, it was perfectly legal, and Pablo never felt any guilt about refusing to serve in what he believed were wars of oppression.

The money he had to pay to stay out of the army had cost Casals most of his savings, so he turned to other ways to make more money. With his friend from

The monastery at Montserrat, where Casals's music was first published, still performs his music as part of its services.

his Café Tost days, the pianist Enrique Granados, and a violinist named Mathieu Crickboom, he formed a trio that began to give concerts regularly in and around Barcelona. In 1897, he was invited to play in a small orchestra at the summer resort of Espinho, on the coast of Portugal, which is just across the border from Spain to the west. Espinho was a popular spot because of its gambling casinos, and it attracted visitors from throughout Europe.

Now that he was twenty-one years old, Casals could travel alone, although Pilar's "heart was on a string" every time he was separated from her.[3] To get to Espinho, Casals had to pass through Madrid, where he took the opportunity to revisit Count de Morphy. Their reunion was a happy one. "He welcomed me as a son," wrote Casals. "It was as if there had never been any difficulty between us."[4] De Morphy arranged a meeting with Queen María Cristina. Casals was warmly greeted by his "second mother," as he came to regard her. She was greatly distressed when he described his experience in Brussels and his difficult days in Paris, and she gave him a sapphire from her bracelet as a token of her sympathy. Casals later had it mounted on the bow of his cello so he would always remember the royal lady who had taken such an interest in him.

In Espinho, Casals's performances were highly successful, and word of his talent spread rapidly through the international community. King Carlos I and Queen Amelia of Portugal invited him to play for them. Casals quickly accepted the invitation and was pleased to add another royal family to the list of his admirers. When he returned to Spain, Queen María Cristina presented him with a valuable cello made by a master craftsman and awarded him another medal. Casals had been brought up by his father to favor a republican form of government over a monarchy, yet now he was as close to kings and queens as any musician since the court musicians of previous centuries. Such divided loyalty did not seem to bother Casals then or throughout his long life.

While in Madrid, Casals gave his first concert with a full symphony orchestra. It was the Madrid Symphony, conducted by Tomás Bretón, one of his old teachers at the Conservatory of Music. He played one of his own favorite pieces, the *Cello Concerto in D Minor* by the French composer Édouard Lalo. Although nervous as always, Casals gave a faultless performance. The audience did not show any special enthusiasm for the young cellist's performance, however. Perhaps they were not quite used to his new technique, or it might have been that they preferred a much more colorful performance. This was an era when solo performers would do practically anything to gain attention, even at the expense of the music. Casals obviously lacked what we now call showmanship. He was small and did not create much of a stir in the audience when he appeared on stage carrying his instrument that appeared larger than he was. Although only in his twenties, he was beginning to lose his hair, so he did not have any long locks to hang down as he coaxed beautiful sounds from the cello. But as one reviewer wrote: "Short of stature, like that of a boy, he is transformed into a giant when he plays."[5] What mattered most to him was the music he was playing, and he sometimes seemed in another world while performing.

An International
Celebrity

While he was playing in Espinho, Casals was heard by the famous American soprano Emma Nevada, who was vacationing there. She was impressed with Casals and invited him to stay at her home in Pierrefonds, outside of Paris, whenever he visited France. In 1899, Casals decided to give Paris another try and took Emma Nevada up on her offer. When he showed up at her home, he learned that she was about to journey to London for a series of singing engagements. She urged Casals to accompany her; he agreed, and the whole party set out for England. In

London, Casals was invited to play at small, private concerts given at society people's homes. Nevada made arrangements for Casals to make his London debut at the Crystal Palace, a large glass structure that had been built for England's Great Exhibition of 1851. Casals played the Saint-Saëns *Cello Concerto* with an orchestra conducted by August Manns. Queen Victoria was very interested in music, and her aides were always on the lookout for talented musicians to entertain her. One of her assistants heard Pablo at the Crystal Palace and asked him if he would like to play for the queen. Casals readily agreed and traveled to the queen's summer home on the Isle of Wight, off the southern coast of England. There Casals performed before an audience that included the queen and her two sons—the prince of Wales, who was soon to become Edward VII, and the duke of York, who was later to become King George V. After the concert, the queen chatted with Casals in French, telling him that she had heard about him from Queen María Cristina of Spain. The queen found his playing delightful, as she later described it in a telegram to Queen María Cristina.[1] Casals, the dedicated republican, now had the unofficial endorsement of the queen of Spain, the king of Portugal, the queen of England, and two future kings of England.

Casals still had to make his mark on Paris, and he went there directly after his appearances in England.

Carrying a letter from Count de Morphy, he made an appointment with Charles Lamoureux, who was then thought to be one of the most important conductors in France. He was so famous that he had his own orchestra named after him. Casals was shown into the study of the aged conductor, who was studying a score for *Tristan and Isolde*, the opera by Richard Wagner that Lamoureux was about to conduct in Paris for the first time. Casals very respectfully introduced himself and said that he was there only to deliver a letter of introduction from Count de Morphy. Lamoureux read the letter and then said, "Come tomorrow morning, young man, and bring your cello," and went back to studying his score. The next day Casals arrived and once again introduced himself. Seeing that Lamoureux was again busy studying his score, he excused himself and began to leave.

"Young man," said Lamoureux, "I like you. Play for me." Casals began to play the Lalo concerto from memory. Lamoureux looked up from his score and listened intently until Casals had finished the movement he was playing. There were tears in his eyes. "My dear boy," he said, "you are one of the elect."[2]

Lamoureux acted swiftly to introduce the young cellist to the Parisian public. On November 12, 1899, he led his orchestra with Pablo Casals as soloist in the same Lalo *Cello Concerto* before a large and enthusiastic audience. The concert was repeated and received glowing reviews. These concerts made Casals famous "almost overnight," as he said later. "I was besieged with requests to play at concerts and recitals. Suddenly all doors were open to me."[3]

Unfortunately, the man who had opened the first door for Casals was not able to share his success. Count de Morphy died in Switzerland a few weeks before the concerts. He had been forced to leave Madrid because of "certain difficulties at the court," as Casals later put it. "I later learned that this noble person had died in virtual poverty. His death filled me with grief."[4]

Casals left Paris to return home to celebrate his birthday and the birth of the new century with his family. He arrived in Barcelona on December 22, 1899, only to learn that Charles Lamoureux had also died. Casals was suddenly left without a patron and without a champion to further his career.

The nineteenth century ended on a sad note not only for Casals but for his beloved Catalonia as well. For many years, Spain had been fighting rebel forces in Cuba. In December 1897, the battleship U.S.S. *Maine*, which was in Cuba to protect American interests, was blown up in Havana's harbor. Two hundred sixty-six people were killed, and their deaths were blamed on the Spanish Army. The United States declared war on Spain and within a few months had defeated Spanish fleets in the Philippine Islands and the Caribbean Sea

In 1892, Casals was twenty-two years old. It was about this time that he made his concert debut in Paris.

and had won decisive battles in Cuba. The peace treaty between Spain and the United States was signed in Paris on December 10, 1898. Cuba became an independent nation; the United States gained control of Puerto Rico, Guam, and the Philippine Islands. Spanish soldiers had been fighting abroad for years, but hardly anyone in Spain had realized what heavy losses had occurred. Shortly after the war ended, ships carrying what was left of the Spanish colonial armies began arriving in Barcelona. Casals witnessed "thousands of soldiers—the sick, the maimed, and those ravaged by hunger and disease" wandering through the streets. "The horror of it!" he said later. "And for what, I asked myself, for what?"[5]

Now that Spain no longer had colonies to supply it with goods and to purchase its exports exclusively, the country's economy began to worsen. In Catalonia, the anarchists and liberals who opposed the Spanish government gained the support of the people and began to renew their demands for independence. As the new century dawned, the population of Spain did not look forward to the glowing century that the rest of the world greeted with hope.

Casals decided that if he was to make his mark in music, he must do it now. He was twenty-three years old, rather late in life for a solo performer on an unpopular instrument to begin a concert career. He knew that if he was to make it at all, it would have to be in Paris.[6] He left Vendrell for Paris early in 1900 and checked into an inexpensive hotel in the Montmartre section where many artists lived and worked. With Lamoureux gone, he was no longer able to count on appearances with well-known orchestras, but his earlier successes had made an impression on Parisian musical society. He was invited to perform in salons throughout the city, and there he met many important and influential people. A wealthy British woman named Betina Ram heard him play at a salon; when she heard that he was living in a shabby hotel room in the artists' quarter, she invited him to stay at her house.

It was at this time that Casals met Harold Bauer, a fine pianist with whom he had much in common besides music, including a love of tennis. The two practiced music together and appeared in joint concerts in Spain and Portugal, wherever they could find invitations to play. It was the beginning of a lifelong friendship that would result in more than twenty years of joint music-making. Some of the houses where Casals performed were political as well as musical salons, and there he met many reformers, socialists, and supporters of republicanism. Casals, through the influence of his father, fit right in with this liberal group.

In 1901, Emma Nevada invited Casals to accompany her and her husband on a tour of the United States. The United States was then not a cultural center on a par with Europe, and appearances there would not bring him much fame or prestige. Yet Casals jumped at the chance to visit America. Here was the chance to do something new, in a new land, in a new century.

Nevada's touring group was made up of her husband, Casals, and a young pianist named Léon Moreau. They arrived by ship in New York on November 16, 1901. Their first performances were in Massachusetts and Pennsylvania. Nevada was the star, of course, with Moreau accompanying her on the piano. She sang selections from opera and favorite popular songs such as "Home Sweet Home." Before and between her appearances, Casals and Moreau would play solos and duets and sometimes join local musicians in performing instrumental favorites. Pablo did not attract much attention, perhaps again because of his lack of showmanship. He concentrated on the music.

Like most Europeans of the time. Casals was fascinated with the United States. "Newness," he said, "abounded on all sides. One sensed a nation still in the process of coming into being, like a great symphony orchestra in rehearsal."[7] Casals did not confine himself to the company of the rich patrons who attended their concerts. Whenever he had the chance, he mixed with and talked to the laborers and poor immigrants who seemed to fill the overcrowded streets of the eastern cities. In Wilkes-Barre, Pennsylvania, he and Moreau went down a coal mining shaft to experience the daily life of the workers in the mines. They remained so long that they did not have a chance to clean up before the concert and appeared on stage covered with coal dust.

In search of local color in Texas, Casals and Moreau got into a dice game in a frontier town saloon. Casals hit a winning streak and soon found himself in a tense situation. He seldom drank alcohol, and it appeared that the local custom was to down drinks after a winning pass. As Casals continued to win, some of his fellow gamblers took offense. Many of them wore gun belts and looked as though they wouldn't hesitate to use them. "In Texas, we gamble and drink," one of them growled. Luckily for Casals, as he recounted later, he started losing, and the game ended peacefully.[8] In New Mexico, which was then still a territory and not a state, Casals and Moreau went on a walking trip in the desert and came upon a lonely cabin. Casals noticed that the man who greeted them had a familiar accent, and Casals asked where he came from. "Oh," said the man, who was dressed in the broad-brimmed hat and the working clothes of a cowboy, "it's a country you never heard of . . . Catalonia."[9]

The tour ended for Casals in San Francisco. One day he and a group of friends decided to take some time off to enjoy the breathtaking view of the Bay Area from Mount Tamalpais across from the city. When he and his companions were coming down from the mountain, a large boulder came crashing down from above. Luckily, Casals managed to dodge out of its way, but the rock hit his hand and damaged it severely. As he and his friends examined his crushed hand, Casals's reaction was very strange: "Thank God," he said to himself, "I'll never have to play the cello again!"[10] Perhaps he was in shock, or perhaps he was relieved that he would no longer have to live the exhausting life of a touring musician. "If one decides to play an instrument conscientiously with all seriousness, one becomes a slave for life," he said later.[11] He thought that now he could devote himself to the writing of music, which had been his first love, and to conducting. Also, he would be free of the stage fright that had made him uncomfortable from the beginning of his career.

Nevada's tour had to continue without him, and Casals stayed in San Francisco as a guest at the home of Michael Stein, a wealthy businessman. Casals became friends with Stein's younger sister, Gertrude, who was later to become famous as a writer after she moved to Paris.

Casals's hand healed after a few months, thanks to the exercises he performed daily to strengthen his fingers. In the spring of 1902, he was able to return to Spain. After a visit with his family, he returned to his concert career in order to make up for his long layoff.

By this time, he was known throughout Europe, and invitations to perform poured in. One of the reasons for his popularity was that he began to perform Bach's *Suites for Unaccompanied Cello,* which created much interest in musical circles. It appeared that everyone wanted to hear the young cellist play this difficult and unfamiliar music.

Casals and Harold Bauer appeared in concerts throughout Europe and then made a trip to South America in 1903. Casals was now an international artist, and when he returned to the United States in 1904, it was as a soloist, not as an accompanist for some other artist. He was now so well-known that he was invited to play at the White House by the wife of President Theodore Roosevelt. On January 15, 1904, Casals played before the president and four hundred invited guests in the East Room of the White House.

When Casals returned to Europe, he decided to settle permanently in Paris. He moved out of the boardinghouse where he usually stayed and rented a house where he could rest between engagements and practice his art in private. However, the house soon became a gathering place for friends and visiting musicians. This was to become a pattern in Casals's life: a house crowded with people, while Casals quietly practiced at the piano or cello.

Casals made a second tour of South America and then resumed his tours of Europe. Wherever he went, he was sought out by other musicians and musical patrons or just plain lovers of music. In Belgium, he was once more sought after by royalty, and he met and became good friends with Queen Elisabeth, who remained a lifelong supporter of Casals in his musical efforts. He also met and became friends with the violinist Eugéne Ysaÿe, who was also to become a lifelong friend.

In late 1905, Casals toured Russia, which was then experiencing political troubles resulting from Russia's war with Japan in 1904. Returning soldiers were joining striking workers in demanding higher wages and better working conditions. Casals was struck by the difference between the wealthy, elegantly dressed people he played for in the concert halls and the struggling working people he saw outside in the streets.

When he returned from Russia, Casals decided to form a trio with two musician friends. One was the French violinist Jacques Thibaud and the other the Swiss pianist Alfred Cortot. The trio were to play together for the next thirty years in concerts throughout the world. Casals had always felt more comfortable playing with other musicians—it seemed to free him from the terrible stage fright he always felt as a soloist. This may have accounted in part for the long life of the trio and for their ease in playing together.

Members of royalty often requested a performance from Casals. Among them was Queen Elisabeth of Belgium, who became a great friend and supporter of Casals.

With all of his touring and his international celebrity, Casals had never forgotten his family or his native Catalonia. He made regular visits to Spain and purchased some property on the beach at San Salvador, where he had spent vacations with his family as a boy. He intended someday to build a permanent home there. His father's health was getting worse, so Casals bought him a home outside of Vendrell where he could rest and regain his strength. Casals's mother had more time to devote to her husband and other children now that her eldest son appeared to be out of harm's way and able to take care of himself.

In 1906, the trio of Casals, Thibaud, and Cortot decided to open a new music school in Paris. It was called the École Normale de Musique. Soon it attracted some of the finest students from around the world. Casals had always encouraged young musicians and had tried to improve the conditions under which they worked. In Brussels, Casals had once refused to perform unless the musicians were paid for rehearsal time. It was then the practice for concert promoters to allow the public to attend rehearsals, for which tickets were sold. Casals believed that all musicians should be paid for any performance given before a paying audience. Now, most orchestras pay their musicians for rehearsals.

At the school, Casals gave special classes for advanced students, and he always gave special attention to those he thought had unusual talent. A young Portuguese cellist named Guilhermina Suggia was such a student. She had been playing in public since the age of seven and had made her debut as a soloist in 1906 at the age of seventeen. Casals made her his protégé, giving her private lessons whenever he had the time. When Suggia's father suddenly died, she could no longer afford to attend the school. Casals took her under his wing and invited her to stay at his Paris house, where she could be looked after by his housekeeper.

Casals was away much of the time on tour, but when he returned home, he always had time for lessons with Suggia. Soon they were traveling and performing together. Casals and Suggia were very close for seven years, and there even have been rumors that they were married, but these have never been proven to be true.

In 1912, Casals and Suggia decided to go their separate ways, and Pablo began a period of touring and performing that was busier than any before. He gave concerts all over the world in every important city. "I lost track of the number of concerts I gave," he said later. "I do know it was often around two hundred and fifty a year. . . . It was a demanding schedule. I never missed an engagement. I had a strong constitution, but even so I sometimes felt exhausted."[12] It was time for a rest, and he decided to return to Catalonia.

HOME, MARRIAGE, AND WAR

Casals's father had died in 1908, and Casals was now the head of the family. He built a house on the beach at San Salvador and soon became a familiar local figure. In a short time, his house became filled with relatives and friends. He gradually expanded the house and built additional buildings on his land until it became a large estate. It was called Villa Casals and it is still a landmark in San Salvador. He helped his brothers Luis and Enrique avoid the dreaded army service and became the protector of his growing brood of nieces and nephews. He still maintained a busy performing schedule, but he returned to San Salvador every summer. Although the house was usually filled with people, he practiced every morning on his father's old piano and read musical scores and planned his programs during the day. For relaxation, he rode his black horse Florian along the beach, took walks by himself or with one of his nieces, and played tennis, which had become his favorite sport.

Casals was now a celebrity, attracting many admirers. After a concert in Berlin, Germany, in 1913, he met for the second time a young American singer named Susan Metcalfe. They had appeared together at a concert in New York and had written a few letters to each other since then. Metcalfe was preparing a program and Casals agreed to help her with some Spanish songs. He worked closely with her, just as he had worked closely with Guilhermina Suggia. This time, however, Casals got married.

Susan Metcalfe was the daughter of a wealthy physician and had been educated in Europe. She was a serious musician, but she was also well-off and did not have to lead the hectic life of a touring artist like Casals. They were married in New Rochelle, New York, on April 4, 1914. Casals traveled from Paris to New Rochelle for the ceremony and then promptly returned to Paris to resume his concert career. The couple had little in common except their love of music, and their relationship soon became cool. Casals often accompanied Metcalfe when she sang, but critics often spent more time praising Casals's playing than Metcalfe's singing. No doubt this put a strain on a marriage that was based almost entirely on the performance of music.

In the late summer of 1914, war broke out between Germany and western Europe when German forces invaded Belgium. England and Russia soon joined with France to form the Grand Alliance, which began an all-out war against German aggression. Casals and Metcalfe had already decided to move to London before France too was invaded by Germany. There he became concerned about his friends who had remained in Europe, especially Queen Elisabeth of Belgium. He later learned that she had refused to leave Belgium and that she had joined up with the Belgian Army, serving as a nurse. She later set up a hospital and served there throughout the war, caring for the sick and wounded. Casals said of her that "she had an inner nobility."[1] As the war became worse and tales of bloodshed and death reached London, Casals wondered, "Was this what man was created for?" He felt hopeless in the face of such senseless horror. "But," he said, "in the midst of the war's madness, it was perhaps mainly through music that I maintained my sanity."[2] Music remained for him a reminder of the beauty that mankind could produce.

This photograph shows Casals in 1918, about the time of his
marriage to Susan Metcalfe.

As the war became worse, Casals decided to move to New York, where many European artists had taken refuge. He was pleased to learn that his old partner Harold Bauer was there, along with many other old friends. He was warmly welcomed by the refugee artists and soon he resumed his concert career in the United States. For two years, he toured with the Austrian violinist Fritz Kreisler, with whom he had toured in Europe during happier days, and with other musicians. The audiences and the critics loved him, and Casals became as famous in the United States as he had been in Europe.

Casals's good friend Enrique Granados had come to the United States in 1916 for the premiere of his opera *Goyescas* at the Metropolitan Opera in New York. Both Casals and Granados regretted that Count de Morphy could not have been there to see and hear the first truly Spanish grand opera. Granados had planned to return to Spain immediately after the premiere, but he was invited by President Woodrow Wilson to visit and perform at the White House. Granados stayed over for the performance and left for Spain on the next available ship. The ship was torpedoed by a German submarine, and the forty-eight-year-old composer lost his life.

The United States entered the war against Germany in 1917. The country was immediately swept with anti-German feeling, and some music societies refused to

Here, Casals is examining a score with his friend, composer Enrique Granados, in Barcelona, about 1892. He would later help Granados prepare an opera for performance before his friend's tragic death in 1916.

play the work of German composers. Casals put an end to what he considered foolishness by joining with other musicians in forming the Beethoven Association of New York, which continued to play the works of the great German masters.

The war ended in November of 1918, and Casals was anxious to return to Catalonia. Metcalfe, however, wanted to remain in the United States. She finally agreed to go to Spain, but when they arrived in San Salvador, she said she disliked the place and complained about the climate. This was a shock to Casals, for whom Catalonia and San Salvador seemed like heaven on earth. This put a further strain on their marriage, although they remained closely connected musically. Casals and Metcalfe stayed married for thirty-four years, and there was never any talk of divorce. In 1928, however, they decided to live apart from each other. From then on, Casals refused to discuss his personal affairs.

Casals returned to Paris only to find that all of his possessions had either disappeared or were damaged during the war. All of his papers were gone, including valued letters from famous composers and artists he had known before the war. Casals began to give concert tours again and was shocked at the destruction the war had caused in Europe. Many of the cities were in ruins, and wounded and unemployed former soldiers wandered the streets. There was a sense of bitterness

The American singer Susan Metcalfe was Casals's wife of
thirty-four years.

and hopelessness everywhere. Casals hoped that he could relieve some of this suffering and discouragement with his music. He was a firm believer in the uplifting power of music, and he vowed that he would do all he could to bring it to the people—all the people, and not just the privileged audiences of the concert halls.

CONDUCTOR,
PATRON,
AND PATRIOT

In 1919, Casals returned once again to Catalonia, intending to make San Salvador his permanent home. Spain had not suffered as much as the rest of Europe during the war. In fact, it had prospered by supplying much-needed raw materials to the warring nations. Barcelona was now one of the major cities of Europe, but it was still far from being a cultural center. This gave Casals an idea. What Barcelona needed was a first-class symphony orchestra equal to those of the great musical centers of Europe.

Casals had sat in on conducting classes at a school in Barcelona and had helped his friend Enrique

Granados prepare his first opera. While on tour he had often been called upon to conduct an accompanying orchestra, and he was experienced at preparing orchestras for concertos, which require a delicate balance between the soloist and the other musicians. He felt fully confident that he could direct an orchestra full time. He wrote to a friend, "If I have been happy scratching away at a cello, how shall I feel when I can possess the greatest of all instruments, the orchestra?"[1]

Barcelona already had two orchestras, but they did not rehearse or perform regularly. Casals offered to play for them and even finance their concerts if they could provide him with first-class musicians and a well-rehearsed orchestra. No one seemed interested. "They kept on saying that it could not be done and that I had been away too long from Catalonia to know the real conditions there," he said later.[2] So Casals decided to form his own orchestra.

One of the few people Casals found who liked his idea was his brother Enrique. Enrique was an excellent violinist who had returned to Spain two years before from South America, where Pablo's mother had sent him to avoid army service. The government had declared an amnesty for draft resisters, and Enrique had become free to come home. He agreed to become assistant conductor and first violinist of the new orchestra. He also conducted auditions for all the musicians that Casals was able to round up.

Casals had agreed to pay any talented musician double the usual wage for an orchestra player. Finally he had assembled eighty-eight players of the quality he demanded. Most of them were amateurs or part-time professionals who had never played in a symphony orchestra, but eventually Pablo and Enrique turned them into experienced players.

The new orchestra was called Orquesta Pau Casals. "Pau" was Catalan for Pablo and also meant "peace," which turned out to be a fitting name for both Casals and the orchestra. It gave its first concert on October 13, 1920. It was not a great success. Most of Barcelona's music patrons did not attend, but the audience that was there cheered loudly. The critics, however, wrote that Casals was a great cellist but not a conductor.

Casals refused to give up. He would not perform without his orchestra, and it soon dawned on people that if they wanted to hear Casals play the cello, they would have to listen to the orchestra too. Casals called upon many of his old friends to appear as soloists. He even persuaded his old friend Eugène Ysaÿe to come out of retirement. Ysaÿe was worried that he would not be able to play again. Casals wrote later:

> I lifted my baton, and he raised his violin to his chin . . . and with the first notes I knew that all was well. . . . The ovation at the end was frenzied. . . . In the dressing room after the concert . . . he kissed my hands and wept, exclaiming "Resurrection!"[3]

This publicity photo of Casals was taken in New York during World War I. After the war, Casals returned to Catalonia.

Since Barcelona was still cool to him, Casals toured with the orchestra throughout the Catalan countryside. He talked with farm workers and union leaders, trying to convince them that working people would respond to great music if only they could hear it. Eventually, the Workingman's Concert Association was formed in 1926. Members were able to attend Sunday afternoon concerts at reasonable prices, and soon performances were being attended by audiences of two thousand working people and their families. The association founded a music school, a choral society, and an orchestra of its own.

Casals's orchestra soon became accepted by Barcelona, and its concerts at the Palace of Music were sold out. Some of this may have been because people wanted to hear the distinguished soloists, conductors, and composers Casals persuaded to come to Barcelona, but there was little doubt that Casals was the reason for the whole enterprise. It had cost him seven years and $300,000 of his own money to make the orchestra a success, but he felt that the expense had been worth it. To him, they had been among the happiest years of his life.

Unfortunately, at this time, the relations between Casals and the royal family of Spain had become strained. When Casals was trying to raise money and gain support for his orchestra, he had appealed to Queen María Cristina for help. Since Catalonia was still demanding independence and was a center of anti-royalist feeling, the queen offered to help only if the orchestra was based in Madrid. Casals refused on the grounds that Madrid already had an orchestra, but he must have been disappointed in her lack of support. Queen Elisabeth of Belgium, in contrast, had given him all the encouragement she could.

In 1929, Casals was invited by Spain's new king, Alfonso XIII, to play his cello at Barcelona's International Exposition. Casals knew the king well from his early days at the Spanish court when he had played music with Alfonso's mother, Queen María Cristina. He hesitated to accept the king's invitation, however, since Alfonso was disliked in Catalonia. When he became king, Alfonso had said that he was the direct heir of the monarch who had taken away the independence of Catalonia. Casals, speaking on behalf of the Catalonian people, had asked the king and his mother to apologize for the remark, but they had refused. At the exposition, when the king arrived, he received only polite applause from the audience. When Casals appeared on stage, he was wildly cheered. Some in the crowd shouted that Pau was their king, not Alfonso. The fact that they used Casals's Catalan name showed how they felt about Spain. The king later said, "Well, Pablo, I want to tell you how happy I was to see how the Catalans love you."[4] The king obviously was not pleased.

Casals was now secure in his position as a musician, an international celebrity, a landowner, and head of a large family. He began to spend more and more time in San Salvador, where he had become a well-loved and familiar figure. His home had become a haven from the frantic world of touring and performing.

PROPHET AND HERMIT

The Great Depression of the 1930s swept through Europe as well as the United States. Unemployment and poverty caused demonstrations, strikes, and riots, and police and soldiers were called upon to use force to put them down. Governments everywhere were called upon to make changes or be removed from office or power. Many people were talking of revolution or the complete destruction of authority. In Spain, the situation was just as bad, and violence and bombings had become frequent. The situation became so serious that King Alfonso was forced

to allow elections for the people to decide whether they wanted a monarchy or a democratic republic. The people chose the republic, and on April 12, 1931, all of Spain, including Catalonia, became free to elect its own officials and pass its own laws.

Unfortunately, Casals's mother had died only a month before the establishment of Spain's Second Republic. An independent Catalonia had been the life-long dream of Pilar and Carlos, a dream passed on to their beloved son Pablo. Now it was a reality, but it was too late for her to see it.

Casals had been horrified by the violence that had brought about the fall of the monarchy, and now he was saddened by the death of his mother. Yet he could not help being happy over the change in government. At last his beloved Catalonia could stand proud and free. The Catalan language could once again be spoken, sung, and taught in the schools. To celebrate the new order of things, he led a concert of his orchestra before a crowd of thousands of people in Barcelona. The concert ended with a performance of Beethoven's Ninth Symphony. The final movement has a large choir singing the German poet Friedrich von Schiller's poem *Ode to Joy*, a tribute to freedom that expressed the feelings of the Catalonian people.

As a result of all these changes, Casals became personally involved in politics for the first time in his life. He began to see that changes could be made if enough people could be convinced that they were necessary and just. He cut down on his touring schedule and devoted more time to his orchestra and to the musical life of Catalonia. He did take time out, however, to travel to Edinburgh, Scotland, in 1934, to accept an honorary degree from the university there. There he met the renowned doctor and philosopher Albert Schweitzer, who was also receiving an honorary degree. Schweitzer was best known to the world as a humanitarian who had given up his medical practice in Europe to found and run a hospital in Africa. He was also a musician and had written a biography of Johann Sebastian Bach. When he heard Casals play some pieces by Bach at a concert, he was delighted. The two men hit it off immediately and became friends for life.

The joy and era of good feeling that had followed the establishment of the new government of Spain soon ended. Although the new government made many reforms, they were still not enough for some people. Workers wanted more money. Farmers wanted more land. Laborers wanted better working conditions. The poor complained that the government favored the rich, and the rich complained that they were being robbed of their privileges and rights. The Catholic Church favored the restoration of the monarchy, and the anarchists believed in no government at all. Catalonia still demanded complete independence, and strikes and riots again disturbed the peace. Troops were ordered by the new government to put down the unrest and violence.

Those who opposed the new government joined forces with those who were still loyal to the king to form a party known as the Fascist Falange. The Fascists, as they were called, later favored government headed by a dictator, an absolute ruler over the lives of a country's people. In 1936, the democratic republicans united with the Catalans who favored self-rule to form a Popular Front to oppose the Fascists. The Fascists and the conservatives united to form a National Front. The lines were clearly drawn: the Popular Front on the left, the National Front on the right. In the election campaign of 1936, the Popular Front scored a decisive victory, and the Republic was once again in power. For a second time, Casals led his orchestra in a performance of Beethoven's Ninth Symphony, witnessed by a cheering crowd.

The leader of the Fascists was General Francisco Franco, who had led many of the government troops in breaking up strikes and firing on demonstrators. He was a firm believer in power being held in the hands of the few, and he was completely opposed to democracy. He was not about to accept the defeat of his party at the hands of the people. The victorious Republic was having its usual troubles with all the dissatisfied factions in Spain. Again, strikes and civil disobedience were tearing portions of the country apart. General

Franco saw this as an opportunity to seize control of the government.

Franco asked for help from the Italian dictator Benito Mussolini. The Spanish monarchy had always been on friendly terms with Italy. In fact, it was Benito Mussolini who offered King Alfonso refuge when he was forced to leave Spain after the election of the Second Spanish Republic. Mussolini consulted with the German dictator Adolf Hitler, and they decided to support General Franco. Both Italy and Germany had large standing armies and were eager to test them and their new weapons, such as tanks and airplanes, in battle.

In July 1936, General Franco led a revolt of the army in Spanish Morocco. In Spain, his allies in the army and Fascist groups attacked Republican forces and institutions connected with the Popular Front. This was the start of the Spanish Civil War, and for the next three years Spain was to be involved in a bloody conflict that was to be only the beginning of nine more years of the worst warfare the world had ever seen.

On July 18, 1936, Casals was rehearsing his orchestra when he received a message from the city government that a Fascist uprising had occurred and that Barcelona was about to be attacked. He was urged to stop the rehearsal and send everyone home to seek their own safety. Casals decided to finish the rehearsal. The piece they were playing was once again

Beethoven's Ninth Symphony. After they had finished, Casals addressed his orchestra: "The day will come when our country is once more at peace. On that day we shall play the Ninth Symphony again."[1] As he left the concert hall, people were piling up sandbags and building barricades in preparation for battle.

Catalonia was loyal to the Republic, and Barcelona was one of the strongholds of the republican cause. It was bombed often by German and Italian aircraft, and the government soon lost control. Chaos reigned in the city, and people suspected of being Fascists were shot on sight. Churches were burned, since all church members were thought to be monarchists. Prisoners were released from prison, since they were all thought to be there because of their politics. As a result, many criminals were put back on the streets. Soon the different parties within the Popular Front were warring with each other instead of Franco.

Casals was one of the most respected men of Catalonia. He pleaded with the government to settle its differences and stop the violence and bloodshed, but he was rebuffed on every side. The government could do nothing. At the headquarters of the anarchists, he was told: "The people are the only law."[2]

On July 12, 1937, Casals led his orchestra in a concert to raise money to aid the victims of the war. It was to be his last concert with his orchestra. He wanted to stay in Barcelona, but his friends persuaded

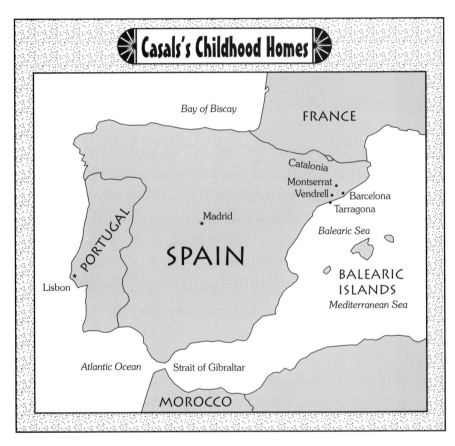

Casals's Childhood Homes

Bay of Biscay

FRANCE

Catalonia
Montserrat
Vendrell • • Barcelona
Tarragona

Madrid

Balearic Sea

SPAIN

BALEARIC
ISLANDS
Mediterranean Sea

Lisbon

PORTUGAL

Atlantic Ocean   Strait of Gibraltar

MOROCCO

This map shows the areas of Spain where Pablo Casals grew up. The Catalonia region, where Casals was born, was a site of bloody conflict in the Spanish Civil War.

him that he could do more good by going abroad and spreading the word about the danger and evil of fascism. Five days later he departed for a tour of South America, which was to be the beginning of his efforts to raise money for the relief of the embattled people of Spain. He gave concerts on many continents, and everywhere he went he spoke for the cause of Republican Spain and the relief of Catalonia. Franco learned of Casals's activities and directed his agents to spread rumors about him. He was called a Communist and an anarchist. Some people actually believed the rumors, and in some cities, he was booed and his concerts were boycotted.

Casals occasionally returned to Spain, but he was warned that it was becoming dangerous for him to appear on Spanish soil. A Spanish general named Queipo de Llano had threatened to take care of him once and for all. "That Pablo Casals!" he had said during a radio broadcast. "I will tell you what I will do to him if I catch him. I will put an end to his agitation. I will cut off his arms—both of them—at the elbow!"[3] Casals took his chances, however.

On October 17, 1938, he gave his last concert in Spain, amid the rubble of Barcelona. It was a benefit for the Children's Aid Society, and the orchestra contained many of his old players. He also made a brief visit to San Salvador and found his Villa Casals filled with refugees from Barcelona.

In despair, he delivered a last broadcast appeal to the world:

> Do not commit the crime of letting the Spanish Republic be murdered. If you allow Hitler to win in Spain, you will be the next victims of his madness. The war will spread to all Europe, to the whole world. Come to the aid of our people.[4]

His words were not heeded, and the world would suffer for it.

Casals was in Paris on December 23, 1938, when he learned of the invasion of Catalonia by Franco's forces. He rushed home as fast as he could but was able to do little to help. Barcelona fell to Franco on January 26, 1939, and Casals was forced to flee across the border into France. Back in Paris, he worried constantly about the fate of his family and friends. He wanted desperately to save them but was warned that it would be suicide to return to Catalonia. Finally a Spanish refugee told him that the Villa Casals had been occupied by the Fascists and that his brothers had fled to Barcelona.

Casals decided to move as close to Catalonia as he could get and from there do all he could to help his friends and family. He set up his headquarters in the French town of Prades, just a few miles from the Spanish border. He settled into the Grand Hotel and began immediately to work at helping the refugees and other victims of the war. His old secretary for his

B arcelona, the city where Casals first became a great musical
figure, fell to Fascist forces in 1939, forcing Casals to flee.

orchestra, a widowed woman named Frasquita Capdevila, had escaped from Spain, and he invited her to join him in Prades. His niece Pilar also joined him there, together with a Catalan poet named Juan Alavedra who had escaped across the border. Together they formed a sort of refugee committee to raise funds and do anything else they could to help the war victims.

In May 1940, the "phony war" between Germany and France and her allies ended when German troops invaded the Netherlands and France. They swept everything before them in a *blitzkrieg* (lightning war) and soon occupied Paris. Casals and his small party fled to Bordeaux. There they hoped to board a ship for South America where Casals knew he could be sheltered by friends. The ship on which they were supposed to sail was sunk before it reached Bordeaux, so they were forced to return to Prades. The Grand Hotel refused to let them back in for fear that the Germans would punish them for sheltering Casals, who was considered an enemy of Germany. Casals was forced to rent a small house called the Villa Colette. Alavedra and his family resided on the first floor, and Casals occupied the upstairs. It was to remain his home for nine years.

When the Germans arrived in Prades, they did not arrest Casals but instead asked him to play for them. They were, after all, a music-loving nation. Casals declined, saying that he no longer played because of ill health.

The Germans stayed for a while, even handling Casals's cello. Casals was enraged, but he kept his silence. When they left, they even asked him for his autograph and took a photograph of him. Casals's only consolation was that he had not played for them.

In fact, Casals did not perform at all during the German occupation of Prades. Instead, he devoted himself to composition, the writing of music, which was something he had done on and off throughout his life. He started a long work based on a poem by Alavedra called *El Pessebre* (The Manger), which he thought of as an ode to peace. There were few pleasures to be found in occupied Prades, and little to eat. Casals was often ill, but he managed to keep himself busy with his composition. He had a radio that was hidden from the Germans, over which he could follow broadcasts of the war news from London. Thus he spent the long years of the German occupation of France.

When the Allies landed in France in June 1944 and the German Army was facing disaster in Russia, the German soldiers were pulled out of Prades to serve at the front.

Throughout World War II, Spain remained neutral, declaring no connection and offering no assistance to either side. It had proved valuable to the Allies since Spain was their only entry into Nazi-occupied Europe and could be used for the coming and going of spies and messengers. Supplies for resistance groups could also be sent into France over Spain's northern borders. Crippled airplanes could also make for Spain rather than try to return to their bases in England or North Africa. The Allies, therefore, had shown no hostility toward the oppressive regime of General Franco.

When Casals heard of this, he was enraged. How could the free nations of the world, who had just won a great victory over fascism, put up with one of the worst Fascists of them all? Must the Spanish people still suffer under fascism when the rest of the world was freed from its oppression?[5]

Casals received requests from all over the world to appear in concerts. He decided on England, and on June 25, 1945, he played with the British Broadcasting Corporation Orchestra to a huge radio audience. Afterward, he spoke to every prominent person he knew and even addressed the House of Commons, trying to persuade them to overthrow the Franco regime. He met with polite refusal, for Franco had made overtures to the nations of the free world by opening his ports to them and allowing them to build airbases that would be invaluable in the growing Cold War with Russia. Casals was so angry that he refused honorary degrees from Oxford and Cambridge and refused to play anymore in England.

When France and the United States also refused to oppose Franco, he vowed that he would never play in any country that recognized the Fascist regime. He even went so far as to say that he would not play *anywhere* as long as Franco was still in power. He announced his decision to the world through countless letters to newspapers and officials, giving as his reason that "someone must remember."[6] He then retired to Prades to dedicate himself to composing, playing the cello for himself or for friends, and teaching the many students who traveled there to study under the master. Casals had earned huge amounts of money during his performing years, and it had all been held in trust in other countries during the war. Now it was mostly gone, and he considered himself poor, like his mother who had always insisted that she was "the wife of a poor man." He moved into a smaller house, which he called *El Cant dels Ocells* (The Song of the Birds), after the Catalan folk song. The Alavedra family returned to Barcelona, but Frasquita Capdevila remained to act as his informal secretary and household manager. The people of Prades called him the "Hermit of Prades," but he was far from alone. There was always a visiting musician, student, or relative around the house.

Musicians from around the world continued to beg Casals to come out of retirement. Alexander Schneider was a Lithuanian violinist who now lived in the United States. He had a long concert career but had recently devoted himself to the study and playing of Bach's *Suites for Unaccompanied Violin*. Obviously, he and Casals had much in common, although they had never met. Schneider made a trip to Prades just to meet Casals, and the two men became friends.

Schneider tried to get Casals to perform again. He suggested that they do something together, something to do with Bach. Again, Casals declined the invitation. On a second trip, Schneider had a brilliant idea. The two hundredth anniversary of Bach's death was approaching. Why didn't they do something to celebrate the event? Perhaps a concert of Bach's music, right there in Prades? Schneider argued that playing in Prades would not mean that Casals had given up his vow to remain silent but would only reinforce his opposition to Franco by having musicians from around the world come to him. Somehow Schneider convinced him, and Casals agreed.

Schneider happily returned to the United States and began rounding up talent for the event. Every musician in the world jumped at the chance to perform with the legendary cellist. Schneider had no trouble in recruiting such well-known musicians as pianists Eugene Istomin and Rudolf Serkin, and violinists Isaac Stern and Joseph Szigeti. There would be Schneider himself, of course, and Casals's old friend pianist Mieczyslaw Horszowski, whom Casals had known since his Paris days in 1910. The orchestra was composed of talented young people, many of them Americans, who had never heard Casals play, and they looked upon it as the chance of a lifetime.

Many people consider the 1950 Bach Festival as the event of the century for classical western music. People from all over the world flocked to the small village of Prades. Queen Elisabeth of Belgium, always faithful to Casals, attended almost every performance. Franco made it a crime for Spanish citizens to attend, but many slipped across the border to hear the master.

Casals was seventy-three years old, and when he stepped to the podium for the first rehearsal, the young musicians in the orchestra knew they were looking at a living legend. "I thank you for coming," said Casals. "I love you. And now, let us begin."[7] Twelve concerts were given over a period of two and one-half weeks, and every one of them was a huge success. They were recorded and can still be heard on records, tapes, and discs. The festival was also what would now be called a media event. It was reported in almost every newspaper in the world, and magazines carried special articles about it for weeks. If there had been portable television and movie cameras then as there are now, it would have been shown around the clock on television.

Schneider and Horszowski argued that such an event should be repeated, since many artists had not had a chance to attend, and many were anxious to fill out their careers by playing with Casals. Besides, the music-loving public was clamoring for more. Casals agreed, and the Bach Festival, soon to be called the Prades Festival, became an annual event.

In 1951, Casals visited Switzerland to attend a performance of parts of his oratorio *El Pessebre*. There he met Dr. Albert Schweitzer for the second time. Until then, the two men had shared an interest in Bach, but now they had other interests in common. Both were deeply committed to peace, but in different ways. Casals believed that protest was the way to combat evil and injustice. Schweitzer believed that creativity was the answer. Apparently Casals's arguments made an impression, for Schweitzer began to actively campaign against the growing arms race between the opponents in the Cold War. Schweitzer may also have had an influence on Pablo, for Casals began to turn his attention away from just Franco and Spain and toward the cause of world peace.

Casals was especially upset over the growing influence of Franco's regime in the free world. The United States had granted Spain a large loan in order to gain permission to build airbases in Spain. The Cold War between Russia and the United States and its allies was growing worse, and strategic bases were needed all around the world. Casals wrote a letter to President Harry Truman protesting the loan, but the loan was given anyway. Casals began to believe that Franco

In this portrait, Casals is holding pages of the score for his oratorio *El Pessebre*.

would never be overthrown and that he would never see his homeland again.

He did see it again, however, but only because he had made a solemn promise. In January 1955, his old and trusted friend and companion Frasquita Capdevila died, and her last wish had been to be buried in Vendrell. Casals crossed the border into Catalonia to attend the burial. He then made the short trip to San Salvador to visit his old home, which held so many happy memories for him. The townspeople thought that he might have come back to stay, but true to his word, he returned to Prades. He was never to return to Spain again.

A NEW LIFE
AND DEDICATION

One of Casals's best and brightest students was a young woman named Marta Montañez. He had been introduced to her in 1951 when she had visited the second Bach Festival with her uncle. She was then fourteen years old. She had been born in Puerto Rico and had been studying the cello from an early age. Casals took an interest in the girl and her uncle because they knew people in Puerto Rico who were related to his mother. Marta played for Casals, and he complimented her on her talent. Casals enjoyed teaching young people who had talent, but he thought it was not wise for such a young girl to study so far from home. He told her uncle that she should first finish her education before beginning any real study of the cello.

Marta and her uncle returned to Puerto Rico, and Marta followed Casals's advice. She had transferred to the Marymount School in New York City after her elementary education in Puerto Rico, and she graduated with honors. In 1954, she was studying the cello in New York when her uncle again asked Casals if he would take her on as a student. Casals agreed, and Marta and her mother traveled to Prades to settle in for lessons from Casals.

Marta was now an attractive and lively young woman of eighteen. Many people thought she resembled Casals's mother. She was very good at languages and was soon assisting Casals with his correspondence and other professional chores. They grew closer and closer together. Each summer, Casals taught cello at the Summer Academy of Music in the Swiss Alps. That summer, he took Marta with him, and he introduced her to Albert Schweitzer and to the actor and film director Charlie Chaplin. They traveled to Belgium, where they visited with Queen Elisabeth, and then to Bonn, Germany, where he showed her Beethoven's birthplace. It was obvious that Marta had become more than a student and assistant to Casals. He was showing her off to his friends.

Casals had never been to Puerto Rico, the home of both his mother and Marta, or Martita as he now called her. For years, musicians and friends from Puerto Rico had urged him to visit their beautiful island, and now he decided to go. Besides, Marta was a little homesick. He and Marta were joined by his brother Enrique and Enrique's wife María, who also wanted to see the birthplace of Pilar Casals. They arrived in San Juan on December 11, 1955. Casals was delighted. "For me, Puerto Rico was a case of love at first sight," he said. "Everything my mother had told me about its beauty I now saw with my own eyes. . . . And what hospitality! Everywhere, I was greeted with flowers."[1]

Casals was also greeted with applause wherever he went. Special events were put on in his honor, and he attended countless banquets and listened to many speeches praising him. He and Martita went to Mayagüez to visit his mother's birthplace, and they discovered that Martita's mother had been born in the same house! Casals was delighted, and the crowd cheered when he played a Catalan lullaby that his mother had taught him. When he met the governor of Puerto Rico, Luis Muñoz Marín, the governor said, "Don Pablo, join us and live here!"[2] Casals was tempted, but he still had responsibilities in Europe.

Casals and Martita returned to Prades in March 1956 for the seventh annual Prades Festival. Before he left Puerto Rico, however, he had agreed to return to oversee a *Festival Casals de Puerto Rico* for the next year. He spent his usual summer in Switzerland at the music school and then went on to Paris to attend a concert in his honor. In November, Casals and Martita left the little house in Prades and departed for Puerto Rico, perhaps never to return.

Pablo celebrated his eightieth birthday on December 29, 1956, in San Juan. Congratulations flowed in from all over the world as well as invitations to visit each of the countries. Many invitations came from the United States, but Casals sadly chose to refuse them, since the government still supported Franco. When it was pointed out that he was now living in what was considered a part of the United States, he said he believed that it made no difference. Puerto Rico "has no voice in foreign affairs," he said, "and is therefore blameless."[3] He and Martita moved into an apartment in San Juan overlooking the beaches and ocean that reminded him of San Salvador.

In the spring of 1957, Casals began to prepare for the upcoming festival, which was to consist of twelve concerts conducted by Casals himself. On April 16, just a week before the festival was to open, he was conducting a rehearsal when he suddenly excused himself. He stepped down from the podium and with great difficulty made his way to his dressing room. He had a sharp pain in his chest and was feeling sick to his stomach. He was having a heart attack! He insisted on going home rather than to a hospital. In the ambulance taking him there, he was heard to mutter, "What a shame . . . such a wonderful orchestra."[4]

Casals insisted that the festival go on without him. The musicians decided to play, but without a conductor, in honor of Casals. Alexander Schneider, the first violinist, led the orchestra from the violin section while the podium remained empty. The festival was a great success, which indicated how the people of Puerto Rico felt about Casals. At Prades, many people had canceled their tickets whenever Pablo was unable to play for some reason.

Many people thought that a man of Casals's age could not survive a heart attack, but survive it he did. One of his exercises on the road to recovery was practicing the cello, which his doctors had warned him not to do. He believed that once more his music had helped him over another obstacle.

On August 3, 1957, Casals and Martita were married. They had been planning to do so for some time, but first Casals had to obtain a divorce from Susan Metcalfe, whom he had not seen for thirty years. There was no trouble with the divorce. Casals was eighty years old, and Martita was twenty-one. Some people were doubtful about the wisdom of the marriage because of the difference in their ages, but that did not bother either of them. Once again, Queen Elisabeth of

Belgium came through: "How happy I am, knowing dear little Martita, to learn that you are both united."[5]

Shortly after the wedding ceremony, Casals and Marta left for Europe, where Casals taught his usual cello course in Switzerland. After winding up some musical and business affairs, they returned to Puerto Rico. They built a beach house in Santurce near San Juan, which was to be Casals's base for a whole new round of activities.

Like Barcelona more than thirty years before, Puerto Rico did not have a first-class symphony orchestra. Casals quickly saw to that, in the same way he had done in Barcelona. He rounded up all the best amateur and professional musicians on the island and convinced his old friends to appear as soloists. He toured the island, just as he had done in Catalonia, bringing great music to people who normally would not attend a concert of classical music. He also became president of the new Conservatory of Music of Puerto Rico, an institution that probably never would have come about without Casals's presence on the island.

Casals's old friend Rudolf Serkin was the director of the Marlboro Music School and Festival in Vermont. It was not like any other festival because its purpose was not to attract audiences and sell tickets. It was more like a gathering of professionals who liked to get together and talk shop and show each other what they

Casals and his wife, Marta, attended a reception in their honor in New York in 1966.

could do. Alexander Schneider suggested that Serkin invite Casals to attend and join in the activities. Casals accepted, since he would not be playing in public. He enjoyed it so much that he became a regular, and he and Marta spent part of each summer there.

In the late 1950s, the Cold War between the United States and its allies and the Soviet Union had reached a point where the danger of actual war was ever present. Both sides were engaged in producing more and deadlier atomic weapons and in building up their armed forces. Albert Schweitzer had become the principal spokesperson for all the people of the world who were horrified at the possibility of nuclear warfare. Schweitzer appealed to his old friend Casals to aid him in bringing more attention to this horrible state of affairs. Casals agreed to play at a special concert celebrating the thirteenth anniversary of the United Nations. He would also make a plea for peace.

The concert took place on October 24, 1958. He and his old friend Mieczyslaw Horszowski played Bach's Sonata No. 2 in D Major for cello and piano. Casals also played the Catalan "Song of the Birds" in memory of the victims of the Spanish Civil War.

Casals had made a recording in four different languages in which he made a plea for world peace. "I wish that there could be a tremendous movement of protest in all countries, and especially from the mothers, that would impress those who have the power to prevent this catastrophe [of nuclear war]."[6] The concert was televised and broadcast to seventy-four nations. Casals had reached as many people with his message of peace as was humanly possible.

RETURN TO CATALONIA

Many people thought that with his concert at the United Nations, Casals had completed his mission in the world of politics. He would not stop, however, and he continued to hound world leaders with letters and statements to the press concerning the situation in Spain. When John F. Kennedy was elected president of the United States in 1960, Casals sent him a letter reminding him of the plight of the people of Spain and how wrong it was for a great country to support an oppressive government. Casals, of course, had sent such a letter to every American president since the end of World War II. This time he received a respectful reply and an invitation to play at the White House. Casals was impressed with the youthful president and believed that here at last was someone who had real power and might listen to him seriously. He decided to accept the invitation, and the resulting concert was one of the cultural high points in the history of the White House.

Casals now had a complete concert version of his oratorio *El Pessebre* ready for performance. Whenever he accepted a request to perform with an orchestra, the management was usually grateful enough to include it in the concert. In this way, Casals spread his "ode to peace" throughout the world. He continued to insist that he had not broken his vow not to perform in any country that still recognized Franco. He considered his performances at the United Nations, at the White House, and at Marlboro as private performances to invited guests. Anyway, if he had broken it, it was strictly in the cause of peace and not for fame or fortune. He had already had plenty of those.

In 1963, Casals was informed that President Kennedy wanted to award him the Presidential Medal of Freedom for his efforts in promoting world peace. Before this could come about, the president was assassinated in Dallas, Texas, on November 22, 1963. Casals honestly believed that the youthful president could have done more than any other world leader to

Pablo Casals (left) conducted violinists Isaac Stern and Alexander Schneider at the United Nations in 1971.

bring about disarmament and world peace. Before the concert at the White House, Casals had had a private talk with the president. He would later write of the experience:

> We spoke about many things, about his experiences and my childhood, about the grievous conditions in the world. I brought up the matter of Spain. I told the President how much I deplored the fact that American military bases had been established in Spain and that Franco was receiving aid from the democratic powers. He listened gravely—his expression reflected his sympathy. . . . In my heart I felt that this man would do all he could for my people.[1]

He had also believed that Kennedy could have prevented the growing conflict in Vietnam by preventing American forces from becoming involved. "What monstrous madness!"[2] Casals said when he heard the news of Kennedy's death.

Casals had not forgotten the thousands of refugees from Franco's Spain who still lived in poverty and exile throughout the world. He continued to write to every world leader to remind them that there were still people in the world who were being kept from their rightful place in their homeland. His letter to President Richard M. Nixon was answered with a brief note from a presidential aide.

In 1971, Casals was again at the United Nations. He had been asked by Secretary General U Thant to

compose a work to celebrate United Nations Day. U
Thant had suggested that he set the Preamble to the
UN Charter to music, but Casals found the language
too formal. The celebrated poet W. H. Auden agreed
to compose an ode for the occasion, and within a few
days, he delivered a forty-three-line poem to Pablo.
Casals composed his *Hymn to the United Nations* and
conducted it himself on October 24, 1971. U Thant
then presented him with the UN Peace Medal.

His last concert was in Israel in September 1973.
Israel had become a favorite stop on his tours since he
had judged a cello competition there in 1966. Before
leaving Israel to return to Puerto Rico, he met with Prime
Minister Golda Meir. He played the cello for her. It may
have been his last performance for anyone. When he
was finished, he said, "My cello is my oldest friend . . .
oh, yes . . . my cello is my companion. I love him and he
loves me. And he sounds well to make me happy."[3]

Back home in Puerto Rico, Casals suffered a second
heart attack while playing dominoes with a friend. At the
hospital, he told the nurses, "Damn it, I will not die!"[4] But
he did, on October 22, 1973, at the age of ninety-six.

The next day a mass was said for him at a small
San Juan church. His own recording of "The Song of
the Birds" was played, and the casket was taken to a
small cemetery in view of the sea he loved so much.

Two years later, in November 1975, Francisco
Franco died. Civil unrest in Spain forced free elections

This photograph shows Pablo Casals performing his *Hymn to the United Nations* in 1971.

in 1977, but it was not until 1979 that Catalonia was at last given the right to govern itself. That year, Casals's casket was removed from the cemetery by the sea, and a farewell mass was said at San Juan Cathedral in Puerto Rico. Marta and several of Casals's friends brought the casket to Barcelona, where it lay in state in the palace. On November 10, 1979, the casket containing Casals's remains was placed in the ground in Vendrell alongside the graves of all the members of his family.

During his lifetime, Pablo Casals's name was often linked with those of the great physicist Albert Einstein and the theologian and philosopher Albert Schweitzer. They were called "the three towering figures of the contemporary world."[5] Einstein was one of the few great men of his era whom Casals had not met, but he most likely would have gotten along with him famously. For all three men had two things in common: a love of music and a passionate desire for peace. Of the three, Pablo Casals had made the greatest sacrifice for the goal of peace. He had stopped doing what he wanted most to do: play the music he loved for the people he loved. Sometimes the most difficult thing to do is to hold back your gifts, but Casals had done it for what he sincerely believed was the betterment of humankind. His legacy was the proposition that peace, like music, will endure so long as people continue to hold it in their hearts and minds and never let it go.

CHRONOLOGY

1876—Pablo Carlos Salvador Casals y Defilló is born on December 29 in Vendrell, Catalonia, Spain.

1887—Casals hears José García play the cello and decides this will be his instrument.

1888—Casals moves to Barcelona and studies cello with García at the Municipal School of Music.

1889—Casals starts playing in Barcelona cafés and is heard by composer Isaac Albéniz, who gives him a letter of introduction to Count de Morphy.

1891—Casals gives his first solo concert.

1892—Casals discovers Bach's *Suites for Unaccompanied Cello.*

1893—After graduating from the Municipal School of Music, Casals moves to Madrid, meets Count de Morphy, plays for the queen of Spain, and receives a royal grant to study at the Madrid Conservatory of Music.

1895—Casals moves to Brussels but refuses to enter the Conservatory of Music and loses royal grant. He then moves to Paris and plays in theater orchestra.

1896—Returning to Barcelona, Casals begins teaching at the Municipal School of Music. He avoids the army by paying officials not to draft him.

1897—Casals forms a trio with Mathieu Crickboom and Enrique Granados and plays at the summer resort of Espinho. He also plays before the king and queen of Portugal and solos with the Madrid Symphony Orchestra.

1899—Casals makes his English debut at London's Crystal Palace, playing for Queen Victoria. He then plays with Lamoureux Orchestra in Paris.

1901—Casals tours the United States with Emma Nevada.

1904—During his second tour of the United States, Casals plays at the White House for President Theodore Roosevelt.

1906—Casals forms a new trio with Jacques Thibaud and Alfred Cortot, and they establish a music school in Paris. He begins a relationship with Guilhermina Suggia.

1912—Casals and Suggia end their relationship.

1914—Susan Metcalfe and Casals are married and move to the United States at outbreak of World War I.

1915—With Fritz Kreisler and other musicians, Casals tours the United States.

1919—Casals returns to Barcelona at the end of the war. There, he forms Orquesta Pau Casals.

1931—Casals conducts Beethoven's Ninth Symphony to celebrate founding of Spain's Second Republic.

1934—Casals is awarded an honorary degree at Edinburgh University and meets Dr. Albert Schweitzer.

1936—Spanish Civil War breaks out. Casals gives his last concert with Orquesta Pau Casals.

1939—Franco takes over in Spain. Casals settles in Prades, France, and continues to work for relief of Spanish refugees. He begins work on the oratorio *El Pessebre.*

1945—Casals resumes cello performances after World War II ends. He continues his anti-Franco campaign from Prades and vows never to play in any country that recognizes Franco's Spain.

1950—With Alexander Schneider, Casals organizes Bach Festival.

1955—Casals begins relationship with Marta Montañez.

1956—Casals and Montañez settle in Puerto Rico.

1957—Casals suffers a heart attack while rehearsing for the Festival Casals. He later forms the Puerto Rico Symphony Orchestra and a musical conservatory. Montañez and Casals marry.

1958—Casals performs at thirteenth anniversary of United Nations.

1961—Casals performs at the White House for President John F. Kennedy and receives assurance that the president will work for world peace.

1962—Casals finishes *El Pessebre* and tours for world peace.

1971—Casals conducts his *Hymn to the United Nations* at the UN.

1973—Casals suffers a second heart attack and dies on October 22. He is buried in Puerto Rico.

1979—Casals's body is returned to Spain after Franco dies and a republic in Spain is established. He is reburied in Vendrell on November 29.

CHAPTER NOTES

CHAPTER 1

1. H.L. Kirk, *Pablo Casals* (New York: Holt, Rinehart & Winston, 1974), pp. 520–521.

2. Paul Henry Lang, *New York Herald Tribune,* November 14, 1961., quoted in Kirk, pp. 520–521.

3. Ibid.

4. Pablo Casals, *Joys and Sorrows: Reflections* (New York: Simon & Schuster, 1970), p. 291.

5. Ibid.

6. Ibid., p. 290.

CHAPTER 2

1. J.M. Corredor, *Conversations with Casals* (New York: Dutton, 1956), p. 15.

2. Pablo Casals, *Joys and Sorrows: Reflections* (New York: Simon & Schuster, 1970), p. 32.

3. Ibid., pp. 33–34.

4. Ibid., p. 35.

5. Robert Baldock, *Pablo Casals* (Boston: Northeastern University Press, 1992), p. 29.

6. Pablo Casals, "The Story of My Youth," *Windsor Magazine,* November 1930, pp. 717–723. Quoted in H.L. Kirk, *Pablo Casals* (New York: Holt, Rinehart & Winston, 1974), p. 60.

7. Louis Biancolli, "Interview with Casals," *McCall's,* May 1966. Quoted in Kirk, p. 67.

CHAPTER 3

1. Pablo Casals, *Joys and Sorrows: Reflections* (New York: Simon & Schuster, 1970), p. 58.

2. J.M. Corredor, *Conversations with Casals* (New York: Dutton, 1956), p. 31.

3. Casals, p. 60.

4. Review from *El Alcance*, September 25, 1894. Quoted in H.L. Kirk, *Pablo Casals* (New York: Holt, Rinehart & Winston, 1974), p. 87.

5. Casals, p. 66.

CHAPTER 4

1. Pablo Casals, *Joys and Sorrows: Reflections* (New York: Simon & Schuster, 1970), pp. 69–70.

2. Hedda Garza, *Pablo Casals* (New York: Chelsea House, 1993), p. 48.

3. Ibid., p. 49.

4. Casals, p. 77.

5. H.L. Kirk, *Pablo Casals* (New York: Holt, Rinehart & Winston, 1974), p. 109.

CHAPTER 5

1. Pablo Casals, *Joys and Sorrows: Reflections* (New York: Simon & Schuster, 1970), p. 88.

2. Ibid., pp. 91–92.

3. Ibid., p. 93.

4. Ibid., p. 92.

5. Ibid., p. 145.

6. H.L. Kirk, *Pablo Casals* (New York: Holt, Rinehart & Winston, 1974), p. 134.

7. Casals, p. 101.

8. Kirk, p. 158.

9. Casals, p. 104.

10. Ibid., p. 105.

11. J.M. Corredor, *Conversations with Casals* (New York: Dutton, 1956), p. 51.

12. Casals, p. 110.

CHAPTER 6

1. Pablo Casals, *Joys and Sorrows: Reflections* (New York: Simon & Schuster, 1970), p. 129.

2. Ibid., p. 147.

CHAPTER 7

1. H.L. Kirk, *Pablo Casals* (New York: Holt, Rinehart & Winston, 1974), pp. 323–324.

2. J.M. Corredor, *Conversations with Casals* (New York: Dutton, 1956), p. 70.
3. Pablo Casals, *Joys and Sorrows: Reflections* (New York: Simon & Schuster, 1970), p. 164.
4. Corredor, p. 79.

CHAPTER 8
1. Pablo Casals, *Joys and Sorrows: Reflections* (New York: Simon & Schuster, 1970), p. 219.
2. Ibid., p. 222.
3. Ibid., p. 226.
4. Ibid., p. 227.
5. Ibid., p. 256.
6. Garza, *Pablo Casals* (New York: Chelsea House, 1993), p. 85.
7. H.L. Kirk, *Pablo Casals* (New York: Holt, Rinehart & Winston, 1974), p. 454.

CHAPTER 9
1. Pablo Casals, *Joys and Sorrows: Reflections* (New York: Simon & Schuster, 1970), pp. 270–271.
2. Ibid., p. 272.
3. H.L. Kirk, *Pablo Casals* (New York: Holt, Rinehart & Winston, 1974), p. 491.
4. Ibid., p. 494.
5. Ibid., p. 499.
6. Ibid., p. 507.

CHAPTER 10
1. Pablo Casals, *Joys and Sorrows: Reflections* (New York: Simon & Schuster, 1970), pp. 290-291.
2. Ibid., p. 294.
3. Robert Baldock, *Pablo Casals* (Boston: Northeastern University Press, 1992), p. 256.
4. Hedda Garza, *Pablo Casals* (New York: Chelsea House, 1993), p. 98.
5. H.L. Kirk, *Pablo Casals* (New York: Holt, Rinehart & Winston, 1974), p. 483.

GLOSSARY

anarchist—A person who believes there should be no government to limit the absolute freedom of the people of a country.

boycott—To refuse to buy or use something, as a form of protest.

concerto—A musical composition for one or more instruments accompanied by a full orchestra.

dictator—A person who has absolute power to run a government and to make laws.

fascism—A system of government led by a dictator who claims absolute control over the people of a country.

monarchist—A person who believes in government headed by a king or queen; also called a royalist.

oratorio—A lengthy musical composition for chorus and orchestra, usually on a religious theme.

patron—An important or wealthy person who supports an artist or craftsperson for the sake of the art or craft.

prodigy—A child or young person with outstanding talent in an art or craft.

protégé—Someone who is guided in his or her career by a wealthy or important person.

republican—A person who believes in government conducted by representatives elected by the people of a country.

suite—A musical composition consisting of short movements or dances.

FURTHER READING

Baldock, Robert. *Pablo Casals.* Boston: Northeastern University Press, 1992.

Casals, Pablo. *Joys and Sorrows: Reflections.* New York: Simon & Schuster, 1970.

Corredor, J.M. *Conversations with Casals.* New York: Dutton, 1956.

Garza, Hedda. *Pablo Casals.* New York: Chelsea House, 1993.

Hargrove, Jim. *Pablo Casals: Cellist of Conscience.* Chicago: Children's Press, 1991.

Kirk, H.L. *Pablo Casals.* New York: Holt, Rinehart & Winston, 1974.

INDEX